# Making More of Holy Week

# Making More of Holy Week

*by Edmund Flood, O.S.B.*

paulist press new york/ramsey

Library of Congress
Catalog Card Number: 83-62472

ISBN: 0-8091-5184-7

Published by Paulist Press,
545 Island Road, Ramsey, N.J. 07446

Printed and bound in the United States of America

# Contents

*Acknowledgments*
A few lines in this book were taken from *Good News Bible, The Bible in Today's English Version,* published by The American Bible Society.

The majority of the Scripture quotations in this publication are from the Revised Standard Version of the Bible, copyrighted 1946, 1952 © 1971, 1973 by the Division of Christian Education of the National Council of Churches of Christ in the U.S.A., and used by permission.

# A Note to the Reader

What do I want from life?

Each of us could make quite a list. We want enough food and drink, freedom from pain, pleasure, companionship, love and so on. Perhaps the greatest difference between them is that some have a transient effect and some can be lasting.

I eat today; and tomorrow and the day after I shall have to eat again. I have pleasure from sport, a beautiful day, or an amusing play. Any of these may have a profound and permanent effect on me; but some can be like flowers that will fade and wither.

Sometimes I ask whether my life is just a succession of experiences, one after another, lapsing at last into nothingness. Is all my striving to be loving, generous, a person of integrity, ultimately to be an exploded bubble, so far as I am concerned?

The question comes to us so poignantly when a close friend dies. As I stand by the grave, I have many memories of happy times we spent together. But a stronger memory still is of a unique person who, in the joys and difficulties of his or her life, hewed out that uniqueness, that trueness to self, which drew my love and reverence. Does *that* become just a carcass?

Holy Week is about that question. It asks whether human life really comes to anything. We catch the force of the question by looking at ourselves and the people we value. And we'll become more aware of the answer by following what happened in the life and death of Jesus and then celebrating what we've found in these services.

This booklet presents Jesus' life and death around four of the main events in his life (his entry into Jerusalem, his last supper with his friends, his death and his resurrection). And it offers a few suggestions how we can make more of the Holy Week services so as to realize and rejoice in what we've found.

# PASSION SUNDAY

## Up to the City

A man on an unimpressive young animal riding up toward a city. Holy Week starts with as stark and moving a contrast as any film.

It was like Duncan coming under the battlements of Macbeth's castle. Jerusalem stood for the religious establishment to whom Jesus had so quickly become an intolerable threat.

But Jerusalem also stood for the people through whom God wanted to bring life to the world. Threat? Or hope for everyone? That was the question raised by the man riding up to the city.

The man was riding, like any religious teacher might, the then equivalent of a clapped-out Ford. He was accompanied by a crowd. Not much of one, probably. A bunch of Galilean provincials like himself. But they'd seen something of this man. He cured people. They'd seen a power in him that could overcome the misery in people's lives. In their towns and villages, men and women they knew had found, through this man, health and joy and hope.

If they'd thought of him just as a specially successful faith-healer, they wouldn't have been cheering him now. But they were Jews. And with all their people their great longing was that God would one day use his full power to give them the kind of life they sometimes glimpsed.

That is a longing in every man and woman—one that we're hardly aware of when the going is smooth, but potentially all-consuming when we face tragedy and death.

What was special about the Jews was that it was more than a longing. They were convinced that the God they had experienced over fourteen centuries would satisfy that longing when he came in his full strength, brought in his "kingdom." That was what had kept them a people. They had come to know him as loving and faithful. He was the God who felt for ordinary human beings in their cares and concerns. The word they kept especially for him, as a kind of sacrosanct trademark, was "compassion."

## Who Was This Man?

Could this ordinary-looking man on that ambling young ass really be the man through whom God was bringing in his kingdom, coming in strength?

2

The crowd with Jesus thought so. The cures and the man himself had convinced them that such an improbable thing was so. And now he was coming up to the capital. He'd said how much he wanted to gather together into one family God's divided people, and now he was approaching their center, with thousands of others, for the greatest feast of their year, the Passover.

What *was* his position—and was it anything like ours?

Some people go through life uncertain what to do. Do I want money or a satisfying job? Will I live mainly for myself or for other people?—and so on. But Jesus knew just what he wanted to do.

He had told his friends what he considered to be the only really satisfying aim: to know the Father as intimate friend, and to share in his transformation of people and the world.

He showed that he knew what he was talking about. He knew that there was a power in himself: a power to heal that transformed person after person from their illness and misery to health and freedom.

But he didn't see this as just a special gift that had happened to come his way. The long-promised time had come, when *the God who made things live* would come in all his power. Through *him* this was happening. The power he knew in himself, in the touch of his fingers and the look in his eyes as he moved among these people could *only* be God's coming to those he loved.

A wind of healing was beginning to blow. The people who felt themselves inadequate, despised or rejected suddenly saw everything differently when they came to know Jesus.

We can tell what it was like to be in his presence by reading his parables. Yes, he was talking in them about the new and fuller presence of God: compassionate, faithful, transmuting. But Jesus' parables were there to help you see that that presence was *here*, available now, offered eagerly to everyone, through him! Had they ever seen compassion and faithfulness like his? Did anyone else make you feel like a new person as he did?

## Rejection

But what if you weren't on his wavelength? An unlimited openness to people and their needs won't make you popular with everyone. It can seem to strike at the very roots of a carefully constructed, comfortable system and call into question the authority of those who live by it. If Jesus was allowed to go on putting the absolute priority of love and openness to people's needs before the law, the whole religious system would crumble like a pack of cards.

The choice must have been entirely clear to Jesus. Either he must back down and quietly forget his conviction that through him God was now coming in strength, or he must raise the flag of the inbreaking kingdom and face the consequences. He was coming up now to Jerusalem because he had decided to raise that flag; and today's Gospel of the Passion describes the consequences of his decision.

Jesus stuck to the end to his conviction that God was fully with him, in spite of the certainty of an imminent and brutal death. Not just his going up to the seat of the establishment at that most sensitive time of the Passover feast, but his whole public life, deliberately raised one question. Is this, as Jesus was claiming, the dawn of God's final victory over all that spoils and breaks up human life, like hatred, prejudice, fear, disease and death, or is it not?

And of course that is the fundamental question for every one of us. What ultimately "works" in our lives: a selfish quest for pleasure, a cautiously balanced compromise, or the option that Jesus backed, of a complete response to people's deepest needs?

What Holy Week does is to help us answer that question. It helps us to see what "works," and how it works, in Jesus' life and ours.


# The Service

**Outline**
*A procession* (if feasible)
*Mass*
Readings at Mass:
1. the suffering servant of God

**4**

2. Jesus becoming a slave, and God "raising" him to be "Lord"
3. the passion of Jesus from Mark's Gospel

## In more detail

### The procession:
We begin by trying to enter, together, into Jesus' situation: the jubilant entry of a king into a city implacably against him.

What must he have felt? (cf. Matthew 23:37)

> O Jerusalem, Jerusalem, killing the prophets and stoning those who are sent to you! How often would I have gathered your children together as a hen gathers her brood under her wings, and you would not![37]

Why did he go on with it?

Have I faced anything like the situation he did?

## The Readings
*1st Reading:*
*The suffering servant of God* (Isaiah 50:4–7)

> The LORD GOD has given me
>     the tongue of those who are taught,
> that I may know how to sustain with
>         a word
>     him that is weary.
> Morning by morning he wakens,
>     he wakens my ear
>     to hear as those who are taught.
>
> [5]The LORD GOD has opened my ear,
>     and I was not rebellious,
>     I turned not backward.

**5**

[6]I gave my back to the smiters,
    and my cheeks to those who
        pulled out the beard;
I hid not my face
    from shame and spitting.

[7]For the LORD GOD helps me;
    therefore I have not been con-
        founded;
therefore I have set my face like a
        flint,
    and I know that I shall not be put
        to shame;
    he who vindicates me is near.

This helps us realize how Jesus felt, and also why he went on with
it—his trust in God:

I set my face like flint;
I know I shall not be shamed.

How important is that? Why should I trust in God? It was certainly
a major motif in all that happened that week.

*2nd Reading:*
*Jesus becoming a slave, and being "raised" to become "LORD"*
(Philippians 2:6–11)

    . . . Christ Jesus, [6]who, though he was in the form of God,
did not count equality with God a thing to be grasped,[7]
but emptied himself, taking the form of a servant, being
born in the likeness of men. [8]And being found in human
form he humbled himself and became obedient unto
death, even death on a cross. [9]Therefore God has highly
exalted him and bestowed on him the name which is
above every name, [10]that at the name of Jesus every
knee should bow, in heaven and on earth and under the

earth, [11]and every tongue confess that Jesus Christ is
LORD, to the glory of God the Father.

This tells us, in miniature, the story of this week. It reminds us that
we need to see these events as a whole: as culminating in Jesus'
resurrection as the light and hope of our lives now. The purpose of
this week is to help us realize that more fully.

*The Gospel:*
*The passion* (Mark 14:1–15:47)

It was now two days before the Passover and the feast of
Unleavened Bread. And the chief priests and the scribes
were seeking how to arrest him by stealth, and kill him;
[2]for they said, "Not during the feast, lest there be a
tumult of the people."
[3]And while he was at Bethany in the house of Simon
the leper, as he sat at table, a woman came with an
alabaster jar of ointment of pure nard, very costly, and
she broke the jar and poured it over his head. [4]But there
were some who said to themselves indignantly, "Why
was the ointment thus wasted? [5]For this ointment might
have been sold for more than three hundred denarii, and
given to the poor." And they reproached her. [6]But Jesus
said, "Let her alone; why do you trouble her? She has
done a beautiful thing to me. [7]For you always have the
poor with you, and whenever you will, you can do good
to them; but you will not always have me. [8]She has done
what she could; she has anointed my body beforehand
for burying. [9]And truly, I say to you, wherever the gospel
is preached in the whole world, what she has done will
be told in memory of her."
[10]Then Judas Iscariot, who was one of the twelve,
went to the chief priests in order to betray him to them.
[11]And when they heard it they were glad, and promised
to give him money. And he sought an opportunity to
betray him.

**7**

¹²And on the first day of Unleavened Bread, when they sacrificed the passover lamb, his disciples said to him, "Where will you have us go and prepare for you to eat the passover?" ¹³And he sent two of his disciples, and said to them, "Go into the city, and a man carrying a jar of water will meet you; follow him, ¹⁴and wherever he enters, say to the householder, 'The Teacher says, Where is my guest room, where I am to eat the passover with my disciples?' ¹⁵And he will show you a large upper room furnished and ready; there prepare for us." ¹⁶And the disciples set out and went to the city, and found it as he had told them; and they prepared the passover.

¹⁷And when it was evening he came with the twelve. ¹⁸And as they were at table eating, Jesus said, "Truly, I say to you, one of you will betray me, one who is eating with me." ¹⁹They began to be sorrowful, and to say to him one after another, "Is it I?" ²⁰He said to them, "It is one of the twelve, one who is dipping bread in the same dish with me. ²¹For the Son of man goes as it is written of him, but woe to that man by whom the Son of man is betrayed! It would have been better for that man if he had not been born."

²²And as they were eating, he took bread, and blessed, and broke it, and gave it to them, and said, "Take; this is my body." ²³And he took a cup, and when he had given thanks he gave it to them, and they all drank of it. ²⁴And he said to them, "This is my blood of the covenant, which is poured out for many. ²⁵Truly, I say to you, I shall not drink again of the fruit of the vine until that day when I drink it new in the kingdom of God."

²⁶And when they had sung a hymn, they went out to the Mount of Olives. ²⁷And Jesus said to them, "You will all fall away; for it is written, 'I will strike the shepherd, and the sheep will be scattered.' ²⁸But after I am raised up, I will go before you to Galilee." ²⁹Peter said to him, "Even though they all fall away, I will not." ³⁰And Jesus said to him, "Truly, I say to you, this very night, before the cock crows twice, you will deny me three times."

³¹But he said vehemently, "If I must die with you, I will not deny you." And they all said the same.

³²And they went to a place which was called Gethsemane; and he said to his disciples, "Sit here, while I pray." ³³And he took with him Peter and James and John, and began to be greatly distressed and troubled. ³⁴And he said to them, "My soul is very sorrowful, even to death; remain here, and watch." ³⁵And going a little farther, he fell on the ground and prayed that, if it were possible, the hour might pass from him. ³⁶And he said, "Abba, Father, all things are possible to thee; remove this cup from me; yet not what I will, but what thou wilt." ³⁷And he came and found them sleeping, and he said to Peter, "Simon, are you asleep? Could you not watch one hour? ³⁸Watch and pray that you may not enter into temptation; the spirit indeed is willing, but the flesh is weak." ³⁹And again he went away and prayed, saying the same words. ⁴⁰And again he came and found them sleeping, for their eyes were very heavy; and they did not know what to answer him. ⁴¹And he came the third time, and said to them, "Are you still sleeping and taking your rest? It is enough; the hour has come; the Son of man is betrayed into the hands of sinners. ⁴²Rise; let us be going; see, my betrayer is at hand."

⁴³And immediately, while he was still speaking, Judas came, one of the twelve, and with him a crowd with swords and clubs, from the chief priests and the scribes and the elders. ⁴⁴Now the betrayer had given them a sign, saying, "The one I shall kiss is the man; seize him and lead him away safely." ⁴⁵And when he came, he went up to him at once, and said, "Master!" And he kissed him. ⁴⁶And they laid hands on him and seized him. ⁴⁷But one of those who stood by drew his sword, and struck the slave of the high priest and cut off his ear. ⁴⁸And Jesus said to them, "Have you come out as against a robber, with swords and clubs to capture me? ⁴⁹Day after day I was with you in the temple teaching, and you did not seize me. But let the scriptures be fulfilled." ⁵⁰And they all forsook him and fled.

⁵¹And a young man followed him, with nothing but a linen cloth about his body; and they seized him, ⁵²but he left the linen cloth and ran away naked.

⁵³And they led Jesus to the high priest; and all the chief priests and the elders and the scribes were assembled. ⁵⁴And Peter had followed him at a distance, right into the courtyard of the high priest; and he was sitting with the guards, and warming himself at the fire. ⁵⁵Now the chief priests and the whole council sought testimony against Jesus to put him to death; but they found none. ⁵⁶For many bore false witness against him, and their witness did not agree. ⁵⁷And some stood up and bore false witness against him, saying, ⁵⁸"We heard him say, 'I will destroy this temple that is made with hands, and in three days I will build another, not made with hands.' " ⁵⁹Yet not even so did their testimony agree. ⁶⁰And the high priest stood up in the midst, and asked Jesus, "Have you no answer to make? What is it that these men testify against you?" ⁶¹But he was silent and made no answer. Again the high priest asked him, "Are you the Christ, the Son of the Blessed?" ⁶²And Jesus said, "I am; and you will see the Son of man sitting at the right hand of Power, and coming with the clouds of heaven." ⁶³And the high

priest tore his mantle, and said, "Why do we still need witnesses? [64]You have heard his blasphemy. What is your decision?" And they all condemned him as deserving death. [65]And some began to spit on him, and to cover his face, and to strike him, saying to him, "Prophesy!" And the guards received him with blows.

[66]And as Peter was below in the courtyard, one of the maids of the high priest came; [67]and seeing Peter warming himself, she looked at him, and said, "You also were with the Nazarene, Jesus." [68]But he denied it, saying, "I neither know nor understand what you mean." And he went out into the gateway. [69]And the maid saw him, and began again to say to the bystanders, "This man is one of them." [70]But again he denied it. And after a little while again the bystanders said to Peter, "Certainly you are one of them; for you are a Galilean." [71]But he began to invoke a curse on himself and to swear, "I do not know this man of whom you speak." [72]And immediately the cock crowed a second time. And Peter remembered how Jesus had said to him, "Before the cock crows twice, you will deny me three times." And he broke down and wept.

## 15

And as soon as it was morning the chief priests, with the elders and scribes, and the whole council held a consultation; and they bound Jesus and led him away and delivered him to Pilate. [2]And Pilate asked him, "Are you the King of the Jews?" And he answered him, "You have said so." [3]And the chief priests accused him of many things. [4]And Pilate again asked him, "Have you no answer to make? See how many charges they bring against you." [5]But Jesus made no further answer, so that Pilate wondered.

[6]Now at the feast he used to release for them one prisoner whom they asked. [7]And among the rebels in

prison, who had committed murder in the insurrection, there was a man called Barabbas. ⁸And the crowd came up and began to ask Pilate to do as he was wont to do for them. ⁹And he answered them, "Do you want me to release for you the King of the Jews?" ¹⁰For he perceived that it was out of envy that the chief priests had delivered him up. ¹¹But the chief priests stirred up the crowd to have him release for them Barabbas instead. ¹²And Pilate again said to them, "Then what shall I do with the man whom you call the King of the Jews?" ¹³And they cried out again, "Crucify him." ¹⁴And Pilate said to them, "Why, what evil has he done?" But they shouted all the more, "Crucify him." ¹⁵So Pilate, wishing to satisfy the crowd, released for them Barabbas; and having scourged Jesus, he delivered him to be crucified.

¹⁶And the soldiers led him away inside the palace (that is, the praetorium); and they called together the whole battalion. ¹⁷And they clothed him in a purple cloak, and plaiting a crown of thorns they put it on him. ¹⁸And they began to salute him, "Hail, King of the Jews!" ¹⁹And they struck his head with a reed, and spat upon him, and they knelt down in homage to him. ²⁰And when they had mocked him, they stripped him of the purple cloak, and put his own clothes on him. And they led him out to crucify him.

²¹And they compelled a passer-by, Simon of Cyrene, who was coming in from the country, the father of Alexander and Rufus, to carry his cross. ²²And they brought him to the place called Golgotha (which means the place of a skull). ²³And they offered him wine mingled with myrrh; but he did not take it. ²⁴And they crucified him, and divided his garments among them, casting lots for them, to decide what each should take. ²⁵And it was the third hour, when they crucified him. ²⁶And the inscription of the charge against him read, "The King of the Jews." ²⁷And with him they crucified two robbers, one on his right and one on his left. ²⁹And those who passed by derided him, wagging their heads,

and saying, "Aha! You who would destroy the temple and built it in three days, ³⁰save yourself, and come down from the cross!" ³¹So also the chief priests mocked him to one another with the scribes, saying, "He saved others; he cannot save himself. ³²Let the Christ, the King of Israel, come down now from the cross, that we may see and believe." Those who were crucified with him also reviled him.

³³And when the sixth hour had come, there was darkness over the whole land until the ninth hour. ³⁴And at the ninth hour Jesus cried with a loud voice, "Eloi, Eloi, lama sabachthani?" which means, "My God, my God, why hast thou forsaken me?" ³⁵And some of the bystanders hearing it said, "Behold, he is calling Elijah." ³⁶And one ran and, filling a sponge full of vinegar, put it on a reed and gave it to him to drink, saying, "Wait, let us see whether Elijah will come to take him down." ³⁷And Jesus uttered a loud cry, and breathed his last. ³⁸And the curtain of the temple was torn in two, from top to bottom. ³⁹And when the centurion, who stood facing him, saw that he thus breathed his last, he said, "Truly this man was the Son of God!"

⁴⁰There were also women looking on from afar, among whom were Mary Magdalene, and Mary the

mother of James the younger and of Joses, and Salome, ⁴¹who, when he was in Galilee, followed him, and ministered to him; and also many other women who came up with him to Jerusalem.

⁴²And when evening had come, since it was the day of Preparation, that is, the day before the sabbath, ⁴³Joseph of Arimathea, a respected member of the council, who was also himself looking for the kingdom of God, took courage and went to Pilate, and asked for the body of Jesus. ⁴⁴And Pilate wondered if he were already dead; and summoning the centurion, he asked him whether he was already dead. ⁴⁵And when he learned from the centurion that he was dead, he granted the body to Joseph. ⁴⁶And he bought a linen shroud, and taking him down, wrapped him in the linen shroud, and laid him in a tomb which had been hewn out of the rock; and he rolled a stone against the door of the tomb. ⁴⁷Mary Magdalene and Mary the mother of Joses saw where he was laid.

We want to reflect on what that journey up to Jerusalem led to. Jesus knew what its consequences for him would be. We think about that decision of his. What does it tell us about him?

## The Eucharist

*Reflections*
(especially for parishes with catechumens)

1. Jesus' journey up to Jerusalem was his decision to commit himself fully to the coming of the kingdom, in spite of there being no apparent chance of success.

This week all of us are reflecting on how Jesus backed that commitment with his life, and on the outcome of that.

The only adequate reason for being a Christian is a belief that, in spite of anything that may happen, God *will* come to us in the fullness of his loving power. A Christian is someone who says: "I believe that, and with all my strength I want it"—just as Jesus did as he went up that steep road to the city.

2. Well before they went with Jesus up to Jerusalem, Jesus' friends had been on a "journey" with him. They traveled with him and ate with him. As they did so, they came to know him better.

What they saw in his healing people, in his offering friendship, in his personality, was the coming into their world of the power of God. In a very real and profound way, those months with him increasingly became a triumphant procession. What *could* be more triumphant than what they saw was in him?

In this parish, this Lent, has *our* journey been like that? Have those already baptized and the elect learned to recognize the presence of Jesus in the Gospels, in each other, in our own selves? Have we come to feel that we've at least begun a journey together: a journey with him that means more to us than anything else?

* Which Gospel reading this Lent has meant most to me? When I look back at it now and reflect on it, what does it say to me at this stage of my journey?

* Where have I especially found the presence of Jesus this Lent in the people on this journey with me? I could reflect on the hope of fruitfulness this gives to our parish. What could I myself learn from such people for *my* life?

Lord Jesus,
give the elect faith, hope and love
that they may live with you always.

(from the Third Scrutiny)

# HOLY THURSDAY

### Jesus' Last Meal

Jesus was in his thirties, at the height of his powers. He believed with all his heart that the Father had called him to give the world hope and healing. And now, with his work hardly begun, death stared him in the face—not as an event in the distant future, but just around the corner.

He must have known for some time that an early death was the likely outcome of what he was doing. Now that it was very close, he had to provide for the future. That would center around his twelve closest friends. With great deliberation, he prepared a meal with them.

Of course there was nothing new in his doing that. Long, intimate meals with all who were willing to accept his friendship had always been typical of him. And, in many respects, this meal

**17**

would be like the others he had had with them. You felt close to each other and at ease. You could share your feelings and concerns. And, in indirect but powerful ways, like his stories, Jesus would let you see a little more the gift he held in his hands for you.

Often Jesus had hinted in the last few years that these meals could be more than they seemed. Indeed, they were warm, happy affairs. But every Jew knew that when God came fully to his people it would be like just such a meal together.

## The Birthday Meal of God's People

Even apart from the danger Jesus faced, this wasn't going to be an ordinary occasion. At our birthdays, the people who care about us show us they're glad we were born. This day was the birthday of the Jewish people. Every year, at this feast of Passover, they celebrated the rescue from Egyptian slavery that had brought them into existence. God had broken the mold of history. In that long, untidy bit of history fourteen hundred years ago, he had shown that people's lives aren't a pointless game of roulette. For the first time men and women were able to perceive that at the heart of everything is a person of wisdom, love and power.

Their birthday celebrations didn't only look back into the past, any more than do yours or mine. The God who had given them existence and freedom then would always be the friend at their side. Ultimately he would rescue them from all that enchains men and women.

The climax of these celebrations was the Passover meal. You had it on this night with your family, in any room you could borrow or hire in Jerusalem. Jesus arranged to have his with his "family": the twelve people he wanted to continue his work.

## The Meal Begins

It's not difficult to reconstruct the scene from the hints the Gospels give us. Like Jesus' ordinary meals with his friends, the atmosphere was informal. Somehow the Jews have always man-

aged to keep even their most sacred occasions from becoming stiff or soulless. The off-the-cuff comment, the chatter of children, even humor, simply underline the fact that it is *people*, not robots, who feel very close, here, to God.

As the sun began going down over the rooftops and pinnacles of Jerusalem, the Passover meal began. Perhaps the first part of Jesus' meal seemed to be going much the same way as Passover suppers in previous years, except for the atmosphere in the room of crisis and foreboding. The grace was said, some preliminary food and drink were taken, and the main meal of lamb was prepared.

Then the custom was that the father of the family would be asked by the youngest person present about the significance of the food they were eating. This would have given Jesus, as "father" of this family, an opportunity to explain that this was not to be just one of the long sequence of annual Passover meals held over the centuries. The era of preparation was over. This meal was about harvest. Harvest brings the joy of ripeness and of shared achievement. After his explanation, and before handing around the bread, Jesus expressed in a eucharistic prayer his wonder and thanks for what God was doing through him.

# A Eucharistic Prayer

Here he was expressing what we can all feel in our own way from time to time. Perhaps we escape from what looked like certain death or injury. Or after a time of disillusionment and aimlessness we fall deeply in love or find a purpose in life. It's as though a huge door has uncannily swung shut on doom and despondency to reveal a new world lying bright before us.

The Passover meal's eucharistic prayer over the unleavened bread—like the one said at Mass—is a cry of wonder, delight and thanks that something has happened to us that shows that *God* is here. The great door has swung; we see that the darkness, however somber, is fleeting; we feel ourselves in the presence of a palpable wisdom and kindness guiding things, a person, a lover, whom we call "God."

A eucharistic prayer, whether in the Mass or in the Passover meal, is about what you see in front of you. In that prayer of the Passover meal, the Jews looked at the land God had given his people. They had tilled it, defended it, lived on it, for so many centuries. It stood as the tangible proof that God cared for them, was real.

In Jesus' time—and for centuries afterward—there was no set of words laid down for this prayer, so we don't know what words Jesus used in his. When he had finished, he would have been expected to pass some bread around in silence. But as he was doing so, he broke that silence with those amazing words: "This is my body, given up for you."


## "This is My Body"

We in the West normally think of "body" as being flesh and bones; but sometimes we give the word a different meaning—"This house I have built *gives body* to my idea of having a cheerful, modern home," for example. "Body" here means giving tangible expression, tangible shape and presence, to how I want my home to be. In my house, my aim has become "embodied" in bricks or timber.

For a Jew your *body* was how you gave tangible shape, expression, embodiment to how *you* wanted to be, and how you wanted to relate to other people. How in fact do you live? How in practice are your aims and ideals embodied in your life? What kind of person really are you?

It was in *this*—Jesus not just as flesh and bones, but as the person he really was—that Jesus was asking his friends to share. They had known him as a person who lived totally for others: always available, always "giving himself up for others," at whatever cost. They had seen the happiness in his eyes as he lived like this: as he cured the sick or welcomed the rejected. They had seen his confidence in his Father, even when the hearts of all seemed closed to him.

## A Meal with His Friends

In the East, a meal has always been thought of as forging enduring bonds of friendship and loyalty between people. These eleven men around the table had so often deepened their relationship with him through leisurely suppers. Both then, and always, it was so typical of Jesus. He wants to meet us especially when we are at our most human, most intimate with others. At a meal with close friends we express how happy we are to be friends and our loyalty to them.

At a meal you can also express *your wanting to share in some purpose.* Together you may be starting some enterprise. You want not just to be friends, but to act as friends and partners in a cause you really care about. We shall see how Jesus' words over the wine made this supper, and our Eucharists, just such a meal.

## A Eucharistic Prayer over the Wine

At the end of the meal the president would say a eucharistic prayer over a cup of wine, which would then be drunk by all. The prayer summed up the whole meal.

Again we don't know the words of Jesus' prayer, but we do know what he said as he handed around the cup.

We've seen that Jesus' way of being with us at his Eucharist is that very human activity of a meal. Over the wine, he took the equally profound human activity of a pact.

You make a pact with someone when you want to do more than just express your intention. In a pact you commit yourself: you stake your own integrity on doing your best to carry out what you say.

The Jews' relationship with God had begun with a pact, or "covenant." At that time they were a loose collection of people without a country and without a future. "You will be my own dear people," God had promised these rootless slaves. "I will give you a land. I will give you happiness and freedom. I will love you always, like a wife, a husband, a bride, a daughter." And it would all be for them: he wanted nothing for himself.

## "My Love for You Will Never End"

At this supper Jesus solemnly renewed that promise. The disciples in the last supper and we in our own Eucharists are like a

group sitting around our great protector's table hearing him loving-
ly renew his pact to befriend us always. That is what we're
involved in here—something so simple and personal:

> Your Creator will be like a husband to you,
> the God of Israel will save you.
> The mountains and hills may crumble,
> but my love for you will never end;
> I will keep for ever my promise of peace.

(Isaiah 54:5, 10)

## A Death as Life-Giving

Jesus made it clear what would bring all this about: his death.
So many times the New Testament writers come back to reflect on
that by recalling that enigmatic portrait of a "devoted servant of
God" painted centuries before by a prophet:

He endured the suffering that should have been ours.
We are healed by the punishment he suffered.
He was put to death for the sins of our people.
He willingly gave his life
and shared the fate of evil men.
He took the place of many sinners
and suffered the punishment they deserved.

(Isaiah 53:4, 8, 12)

In all his actions and aims, Jesus had said "yes" to God's desire to penetrate with his life-giving power into his human nature so as to transform the world. He had said it in his complete openness to people in their lovableness and their needs, in the risks he had taken, the rebuffs he had accepted, the hardships and losses he had endured, and in his intimacy and trust in God.

But to say "yes" to God with his whole human self must mean saying it also with what can be that climax of a human life: the act of dying. "You filled the whole of the rest of my life," he said to his Father. "In spite of my fear, I know you will fill my death too."

# The Service

## Outline

**A Mass.** The priest washes people's feet after or during the Gospel.

## The Readings
*1st Reading:*
How the Jews celebrated at the annual Passover meal: God's rescuing them from slavery and evil, giving them freedom, dignity and independence, and making them a people he would always love. (Exodus 12:1–8, 11–14)

The LORD said to Moses and Aaron in the land of Egypt,
²"This month shall be for you the beginning of months; it

**24**

shall be the first month of the year for you. ³Tell all the congregation of Israel that on the tenth day of this month they shall take every man a lamb according to their fathers' houses, a lamb for a household; ⁴and if the household is too small for a lamb, then a man and his neighbor next to his house shall take according to the number of persons; according to what each can eat you shall make your count for the lamb. ⁵Your lamb shall be without blemish, a male a year old; you shall take it from the sheep or from the goats; ⁶and you shall keep it until the fourteenth day of this month, when the whole assembly of the congragation of Israel shall kill their lambs in the evening. ⁷Then they shall take some of the blood, and put it on the two doorposts and the lintel of the houses in which they eat them. ⁸They shall eat the flesh that night, roasted; with unleavened bread and bitter herbs they shall eat it. . . .

¹¹In this manner you shall eat it: your loins girded, your sandals on your feet, and your staff in your hand; and you shall eat it in haste. It is the LORD'S passover. ¹²For I will pass through the land of Egypt that night, and I will smite all the first-born in the land of Egypt, both man and beast; and on all the gods of Egypt I will execute judgments: I am the LORD. ¹³The blood shall be a sign for you, upon the houses where you are; and when I see the blood, I will pass over you, and no plague shall fall upon you to destroy you, when I smite the land of Egypt.

¹⁴"This day shall be for you a memorial day, and you shall keep it as a feast to the LORD; throughout your generations you shall observe it as an ordinance for ever."

*2nd Reading:*
How the much fuller rescue and intimacy that God had promised is celebrated: first as it was by Jesus, and now as it is at every Eucharist. (1 Corinthians 11:23–26)

23For I received from the Lord what I also delivered to you, that the Lord Jesus on the night when he was betrayed took bread, 24and when he had given thanks, he broke it, and said, "This is my body which is for you. Do this in remembrance of me." 25In the same way also the cup, after supper, saying, "This cup is the new covenant in my blood. Do this, as often as you drink it, in remembrance of me." 26For as often as you eat this bread and drink the cup, you proclaim the LORD's death until he comes.

*The Gospel:*
How are we rescued from the darkness in us? How do we become intimate with God through Jesus? Jesus' whole life shows us the way. This incident highlights that way. How am I responding to this example of Jesus of mutual loving service, for example with my fellow-parishioners? (John 13:1–15)

Now before the feast of the Passover, when Jesus knew that his hour had come to depart out of this world to the Father, having loved his own who were in the world, he loved them to the end. 2And during supper, when the devil had already put it into the heart of Judas Iscariot, Simon's son, to betray him, 3Jesus, knowing that the Father had given all things into his hands, and that he had come from God and was going to God, 4rose from supper, laid aside his garments, and girded himself with a towel. 5Then he poured water into a basin, and began to wash the disciples' feet, and to wipe them with the towel with which he was girded. 6He came to Simon Peter; and Peter said to him, "LORD, do you wash my feet?" 7Jesus answered him, "What I am doing you do not know now, but afterward you will understand." 8Peter said to him, "You shall never wash my feet." Jesus answered him, "If I do not wash you, you have no part in me." 9Simon Peter said to him, "Lord, not my feet only but also my hands and my head!" 10Jesus said to him, "He who has bathed does not need to wash, except for his feet, but he is clean all over; and you are clean, but not all of you." [11]For he knew who was to betray him; that was why he said, "You are not all clean."

[12]When he had washed their feet, and taken his garments, and resumed his place, he said to them, "Do you know what I have done to you? [13]You call me Teacher and LORD; and you are right, for so I am. [14]If I then, your LORD and Teacher, have washed your feet, you also ought to wash one another's feet. [15]For I have given you an example, that you also should do as I have done to you.

## The Eucharist

Obviously this is a special opportunity for us to become more aware of what we are involved in whenever we take part in a Mass:

- Jesus chose a *meal* as his special way of being close to us. Is there anything more we could do to make our parish Masses our meal with him?

- He took for this *the birthday meal of God's people*. Should I live my Christianity more as part of God's people? Do the non-Christians around me need to see such a people? To what extent do they do so at present in my parish?

- Jesus' meal soon came to be called "a Eucharist." Is the Mass for us sufficiently a cry of wonder, delight and thanks? How in practice could it be more that for me?

- *"This is my body, given up for you."* We've seen that this means that Jesus is really present as the kind of person he was and is. Let us ask God to make us more aware of the reality of Jesus' presence with us.

- *"The blood of the new covenant":* a promise of love, faithfulness and protection. We could reflect on this in the light of Isaiah 54:5, 10, quoted in this section.

- *Through Jesus' death.* We could reflect on his complete openness to God's will, to people's needs, and to standing for the values and way of life he believed essential—even to death. The Passover sacrifice brought union with God and union among those taking part as fellow-sharers in God's friendship. Does the Mass foster in me that fellowship with God and with those who share with me in this sacrifice?

*Reflections*
(especially for parishes with catechumens)

1. At the end of a long term, a student walks out of college free! So does a patient after a long time in the hospital! In one way or another, we've all had the experience of suddenly feeling free.

God's relationship with his people began with his giving them freedom—from harsh and degrading slavery. The Jews celebrated that every year at Passover because they believed that what God wanted for them and would give them was total freedom to be their full selves.

That's what we're doing tonight at the Passover supper.

God doesn't treat us like children. He doesn't hand out freedom as adults might hand out candy to kids.

So the elect in this parish have had to make their own decision. Like Israel they were willing to launch out into what for them was unexplored territory. Like Israel, too, they were able to do that only because, even quite early, they had enough trust in God.

Haven't *all* of us—whether already baptized or not—been learning these months about becoming a mature Christian: making our own decision to work with God for people's true freedom?

2. All of us who have been sharing in the progress of the elect should be able to appreciate the fact that Jesus founded his Eucharist *as a meal*.

Our meetings and our ceremonies in the Church had a lot of similarities with his supper. They weren't superficial. We didn't just swap stories and jokes. We took care to figure out what we can

know about God and ourselves. We had plenty of happy times. But that came from our joy at sharing something deep and fruitful, and from our exploring and living that together.

Jesus and his friends did that in the last supper. We're called to do the same in our Sunday Eucharists. Together, as we listen and respond to God's word in the readings, we find what he is doing for us. And *then* we celebrate.

3. The priest washes some people's feet. Perhaps a few blocks away, nurses and doctors are spending long hours struggling with people's illnesses. Families are looking after old or sick relations. Others are helping winos and the homeless.

The priest's action is the Church's way of reminding us of people like those families, nurses, doctors and wino-helpers. Not in order to say to us: "Well, aren't they fine! Let's admire them from a safe distance!" The Church is saying: "Service to people was Jesus' way. If we really want to follow him, it must be our way too."

Again, we've been learning a lot about this during Lent and the months before. Catechists, godparents, sponsors and parishioners have come to meetings, services and social occasions to help the elect in their search and to make them feel more part of the parish family.

When our new members became catechumens, the priest asked the already baptized: "Are you ready to help them to know and follow Christ?" The baptized promised that service. By giving it, each in our own way, we have discovered a lot about Jesus' way.

* What does today's Gospel and the priest's washing these people's feet tell me about Jesus' way of service? I could look at the readings we're having this week about Jesus as servant:

Philippians 2:6–11 (Passion Sunday, 2nd reading)
Isaiah 52:13–53:12 (Good Friday, 1st reading)

* What services to others done by this parish have particularly impressed me? Do I feel that some are inadequate or not offered at all—although within our capacity? When the elect have been baptized, the Church asks that they and the community "move forward together, meditating on the Gospel, sharing in the Eucharist, and performing works of charity." We have seen how wholehearted, warm and practical was Jesus' desire to serve people. What about me?

# GOOD FRIDAY

## Jesus as Threat

At some stage in his public life Jesus realized that his life's work was crumbling into failure. He had come to bring God's people the good news. They were rejecting it.

Some people were drawn to him as a religious leader. People from his home province, Galilee, that hotbed of revolution, could be heard to mutter with regard to him, "king" and "kingdom." But others asked whether he was going to start an insurrection against the Roman occupying power. Would he be upsetting the delicate, and to some convenient, status quo, and draw ruthless Roman reprisals?

Even those who realized that his aims weren't political could see his influence as dangerously subversive. Religion—largely understood as adherence to a religious code of conduct—was, for the Jewish establishment, the nation's one hope. Jesus was setting himself above that code. He apparently didn't require the laborious balancing of precedents that they employed to discover God's will. "Now that I have come there's no longer any need of that," Jesus was saying. "God himself is coming into your lives. My whole life should show you that. God now speaks to you, not through elaborate arguments, but in your hearts, if you will listen to him."

How could the religious leaders brook that fundamental questioning of their authority?


## Facing Death

Jesus foretold his death to his close companions; but how must the future have seemed to him? With all his heart and soul he was committed to bringing in God's kingship. It was what he totally loved and longed for—not as a passing whim or a romantic dream, but arising from his unequaled apprehension of God and the lovableness and need of people.

For some the prospect of their failure can be eased by the hope that success will be achieved later by another. But Jesus knew that he wasn't just announcing the kingdom so that someone else could succeed him as its messenger. He *embodied* the kingship. Its power was alive in him—his healings, his welcoming and friendship, his power to forgive. *Only through him* would it become alive in others. Their fate depended on his. He had a oneness, a kinship, with all men and women. When he died, how could the promise of the kingdom survive?

Well before Good Friday, therefore, Jesus was experiencing the real anguish of our death. Am I—my personality, my achievements—*really* anything?

Only God who directs the contribution of everything toward the splendor of his harvest can know. As man, Jesus could not know directly. Great waves of near despair must have assailed him. But though he couldn't see how total failure could be avoided, he held to his belief that good would triumph in spite of all. In his last supper he had staked down that conviction in the face of all the apparent evidence. "I will never again drink this wine until the day I drink the new wine in the kingdom of God." Yes, somehow the kingdom would come. And he would be there to rejoice at it.

On this, the day of his death, he had to live out that conviction. Obviously that would be that conviction's supreme test. If we compare today's account (from John's Gospel) with that of Mark on Passion Sunday, we notice that John is stressing Jesus' kinglike control. Mark stresses the fear, the great distress, the almost desperate desire that the "cup" of suffering should be taken from him.

## A Short Way with a "King"

What now happened to Jesus had been quite predictable since he decided to come up to Jerusalem. As we have seen, it was the greatest of Jewish days, when nationalistic feelings were at a fever pitch in that forcibly occupied country, and the Roman authorities at their most nervous and watchful.

Pilate, their leader, had ruled Judea, probably for four years. That province was known to be one of the most turbulent areas of the Roman Empire. There was much unrest, and freedom fighters were known to be in training. Already the Romans feared that some revolutionary leader, some claimant to Jewish kingship, would light the spark of revolution. Any hint of that must be faced and put down. And the Roman punishment for sedition was crucifixion.

The Jews considered Pilate's rule an utter barbarity. About two years later his high-handed treatment of them brought him a rebuke from the emperor himself. Four years after that he was sacked for extreme ruthlessness. What chance in that situation, and before that kind of man, had a Galilean provincial, with few legal rights, accused of aiming to be king?

True, he would hardly have looked or sounded like a freedom fighter. But the Jewish establishment was presenting him as a traitor, and even disrespectful acts against the ruler could be counted as treachery.


## He Was Crucified

Jesus himself knew that the punishment for rebellion was crucifixion. As a boy in Nazareth he would have heard how hundreds of "rebels" had been crucified in the mountains around Jerusalem at about the time of his birth, and of other cases since.

The procedure was quite stereotyped.[1] On the journey to the place of execution, the man carried the transverse of his cross. Hung around his neck, or carried in front of him, was a tablet stating his crime. Often a circuitous route was taken, so that more people would see for themselves what happened to rebels and be deterred from that crime.

There would be a crowd at the place of execution, ready to gaze or mock. There the convicted man was undressed and scourged. Then he was laid on the ground and his forearms or his wrists tied or nailed to the bar he had been carrying. This was then raised up to a groove in a pole that was usually already standing there. The feet were tied or nailed to the pole. Since the man "sat" on a peg, which was fixed to the middle of the pole, he could

---

1. I owe almost all the details of the crucifixion to H.R. Weber, *The Cross: Tradition and Interpretation,* SPCK 1979, p.xx.

remain in his agony for hours or even days. With increasing exhaustion, he would be unable to keep upright, in spite of the peg and the tied feet, and gradual asphyxiation would start.

## The Service

So the passion was an ordeal Jesus deliberately incurred. Once his message had been rejected, it was the inevitable consequence of his continuing to trust in God, his love for all people, and his conviction that only through him would they find their salvation. For all that, he faced the pain, the humiliation and the darkness.

**Outline** (not always in this order)
*Prayer*: at first in silence
*Liturgy of the Word*: two readings, then John's passion
*General Intercessions*: prayers for Christians and the whole of the human family
*Veneration of the Cross*
*Communion*: (Mass is never celebrated on this day)

**In more detail**
*Prayer:*
We've seen that the keynote of this week is the passage from death to full life, and even on Good Friday the priest's first prayer speaks of Jesus' death leading to his triumph and ours.

*1st Reading:*
(Isaiah 52:13–53:12)

¹³Behold, my servant shall prosper,
　　he shall be exalted and lifted up,
　　and shall be very high.
¹⁴As many were astonished at him—
　　his appearance was so marred,
　　　　beyond human semblance,
　　and his form beyond that of the
　　　　sons of men—

¹⁵so shall he startle many nations;
kings shall shut their mouths because of him;
for that which has not been told
them they shall see,
and that which they have not
heard they shall understand.

¹Who has believed what we have
heard?
And to whom has the arm of the
LORD been revealed?
²For he grew up before him like a
young plant,
and like a root out of dry ground;
he had no form or comeliness that we
should look at him,
and no beauty that we should
desire him.
³He was despised and rejected by
men;
a man of sorrows, and acquainted
with grief;

and as one from whom men hide
their faces
he was despised, and we esteemed
him not.

⁴Surely he has borne our griefs
and carried our sorrows;
yet we esteemed him stricken,
smitten by God, and afflicted.
⁵But he was wounded for our trans-
gressions,
he was bruised for our iniquities;
upon him was the chastisement that
made us whole,
and with his stripes we are healed.
⁶All we like sheep have gone astray;
we have turned every one to his
own way;
and the LORD has laid on him
the iniquity of us all.

⁷He was oppressed, and he was
afflicted,
yet he opened not his mouth;
like a lamb that is led to the slaugh-
ter,
and like a sheep that before its
shearers is dumb,
so he opened not his mouth.
⁸By oppression and judgment he was
taken away;
and as for his generation, who
considered
that he was cut off out of the land of
the living,
stricken for the transgression of
my people?

⁹And they made his grave with the
        wicked
    and with a rich man in his death,
although he had done no violence,
    and there was no deceit in his
        mouth.

¹⁰Yet it was the will of the LORD to
        bruise him;
    he has put him to grief;
when he makes himself an offering
        for sin,
he shall see his offspring, he shall
        prolong his days;
the will of the LORD shall prosper
        in his hand;
¹¹he shall see the fruit of the travail
        of his soul and be satisfied;
by his knowledge shall the right-
        eous one, my servant,
    make many to be accounted right-
        eous;
    and he shall bear their iniquities.
¹²Therefore I will divide him a portion
        with the great,
    and he shall divide the spoil with
        the strong;
because he poured out his soul to
        death,
    and was numbered with the trans-
        gressors;
yet he bore the sin of many,
    and made intercession for the
        transgressors.


This is about the disfigured man of sorrows. His suffering and
ignominy are vividly portrayed. Yet the very first words of the

reading say that he "will prosper, will be lifted up, will rise to great heights." This is because he had willingly suffered for the sins of others. He wanted to be one with them, in spite of their sinfulness, so as to bring them "salvation."

*2nd Reading:*
(Hebrews 4:4–16; 5:7–9)

4For he has somewhere spoken of the seventh day in this way, "And God rested on the seventh day from all his works." 5And again in this place he said,

"They shall never enter my rest."

6Since therefore it remains for some to enter it, and those who formerly received the good news failed to enter because of disobedience, 7again he sets a certain day, "Today," saying through David so long afterward, in the words already quoted,

"Today, when you hear his voice,

do not harden your hearts."

8For if Joshua had given them rest, God would not speak later of another day. 9So then, there remains a sabbath rest for the people of God; 10for whoever enters God's rest also ceases from his labors as God did from his.

11Let us therefore strive to enter that rest, that no one fall by the same sort of disobedience. 12For the word of God is living and active, sharper than any two-edged sword, piercing to the division of soul and spirit, of joints and marrow, and discerning the thoughts and intentions of the heart. 13And before him no creature is hidden, but all are open and laid bare to the eyes of him with whom we have to do.

14Since then we have a great high priest who has passed through the heavens, Jesus, the Son of God, let us hold fast our confession. 15For we have not a high priest who is unable to sympathize with our weaknesses, but one who in every respect has been tempted as we are, yet without sinning. 16Let us then with confidence draw near to the throne of grace, that we may receive mercy and find grace to help in time of need. . . .

[7]In the days of his flesh, Jesus offered up prayers and supplications, with loud cries and tears, to him who was able to save him from death, and he was heard for his godly fear. [8]Although he was a Son, he learned obedience through what he suffered; [9]and being made perfect he became the source of eternal salvation to all who obey him.

This is an application of the first reading to Christ. One who felt our weaknesses "became for all who obey him the source of eternal salvation."

*The Passion:*
(John 18:1–19:42)

When Jesus had spoken these words he went forth with his disciples across the Kidron valley, where there was a garden, which he and his disciples entered. [2]Now Judas, who betrayed him, also knew the place; for Jesus often met there with his disciples. [3]So Judas, procuring a band of soldiers and some officers from the chief priests and the Pharisees, went there with lanterns and torches and weapons. [4]Then Jesus, knowing all that was to befall him, came forward and said to them, "Whom do you seek?" [5]They answered him, "Jesus of Nazareth." Jesus said to them, "I am he." Judas, who betrayed him, was standing with them. [6]When he said to them, "I am he," they drew back and fell to the ground. [7]Again he asked them, "Whom do you seek?" And they said, "Jesus of Nazareth." [8]Jesus answered, "I told you that I am he; so, if you seek me, let these men go." [9]This was to fulfill the word which he had spoken, "Of those whom thou gavest me I lost not one." [10]Then Simon Peter, having a sword, drew it and struck the high priest's slave and cut off his right ear. The slave's name was Malchus. [11]Jesus said to

Peter, "Put your sword into its sheath; shall I not drink the cup which the Father has given me?"

So the band of soldiers and their captain and the officers of the Jews seized Jesus and bound him. [13]First they led him to Annas; for he was the father-in-law of Caiaphas, who was high priest that year. [14]It was Caiaphas who had given counsel to the Jews that it was expedient that one man should die for the people.

Simon Peter followed Jesus, and so did another disciple. As this disciple was known to the high priest, he entered the court of the high priest along with Jesus, [16]while Peter stood outside at the door. So the other disciple, who was known to the high priest, went out and spoke to the maid who kept the door, and brought Peter in. [17]The maid who kept the door said to Peter, "Are not you also one of this man's disciples?" He said, "I am not." [18]Now the servants and officers had made a charcoal fire, because it was cold, and they were standing and warming themselves; Peter also was with them, standing and warming himself.

The high priest then questioned Jesus about his disciples and his teaching. [20]Jesus answered him, "I have spoken openly to the world; I have always taught in synagogues and in the temple, where all Jews come together; I have said nothing secretly. [21]Why do you ask me? Ask those who have heard me, what I said to them; they know what I said." [22]When he had said this, one of the officers standing by struck Jesus with his hand, saying, "Is that how you answer the high priest?" [23]Jesus answered him, "If I have spoken wrongly, bear witness to the wrong; but if I have spoken rightly, why do you strike me?" [24]Annas then sent him bound to Caiaphas the high priest.

Now Simon Peter was standing and warming himself. They said to him, "Are not you also one of his disciples?" He denied it and said, "I am not." [26]One of the servants of the high priest, a kinsman of the man whose ear Peter had cut off, asked, "Did I not see you in the garden with him?" ²⁷Peter again denied it; and at once the cock crowed.

²⁸Then they led Jesus from the house of Caiaphas to the praetorium. It was early. They themselves did not enter the praetorium, so that they might not be defiled, but might eat the passover. ²⁹So Pilate went out to them and said, "What accusation do you bring against this man?" ³⁰They answered him, "If this man were not an evildoer, we would not have handed him over." ³¹Pilate said to them, "Take him yourselves and judge him by your own law." The Jews said to him, "It is not lawful for us to put any man to death." ³²This was to fulfil the word which Jesus had spoken to show by what death he was to die.

³³Pilate entered the praetorium again and called Jesus and said to him, "Are you the King of the Jews?" ³⁴Jesus answered, "Do you say this of your own accord, or did others say it to you about me?" ³⁵Pilate answered, "Am I a Jew? Your own nation and the chief priests have handed you over to me; what have you done?" ³⁶Jesus answered, "My kingship is not of this world; if my kingship were of this world, my servants would fight, that I might not be handed over to the Jews; but my kingship is not from the world." ³⁷Pilate said to him, "So you are a king?" Jesus answered, "You say that I am a king. For this I was born, and for this I have come into the world, to bear witness to the truth. Every one who is of the truth hears my voice." ³⁸Pilate said to him, "What is truth?"

After he had said this, he went out to the Jews again, and told them, "I find no crime in him. ³⁹But you have a custom that I should release one man for you at the Passover; will you have me release for you the King of the Jews?" ⁴⁰They cried out again, "Not this man, but Barabbas!" Now Barabbas was a robber.

19

Then Pilate took Jesus and scourged him. ²And the soldiers plaited a crown of thorns, and put it on his head, and arrayed him in a purple robe; ³they came up to him, saying, "Hail, King of the Jews!" and struck him with their hands. ⁴Pilate went out again, and said to them, "Behold, I am bringing him out to you, that you may know that I find no crime in him." ⁵So Jesus came out, wearing the crown of thorns and the purple robe. Pilate said to them, "Here is the man!" ⁶When the chief priests and the officers saw him, they cried out, "Crucify him, crucify him!" Pilate said to them, "Take him yourselves and crucify him, for I find no crime in him." ⁷The Jews answered him, "We have a law, and by that law he ought to die, because he has made himself the Son of God." ⁸When Pilate heard these words, he was the more afraid; ⁹he entered the praetorium again and said to Jesus, "Where are you from?" But Jesus gave no answer. ¹⁰Pilate therefore said to him, "You will not speak to me? Do you not know that I have power to release you, and power to crucify you?" ¹¹Jesus answered him, "You would have no power over me unless it had been given you from above; therefore he who delivered me to you has the greater sin."

¹²Upon this Pilate sought to release him, but the Jews cried out, "If you release this man, you are not Caesar's friend; every one who makes himself a king sets himself against Caesar." ¹³When Pilate heard these words, he brought Jesus out and sat down on the judgment seat at a place called The Pavement, and in Hebrew, Gabbatha. ¹⁴Now it was the day of Preparation of the Passover; it was about the sixth hour. He said to the Jews, "Here is your King!" ¹⁵They cried out, "Away with him, away with him, crucify him!" Pilate said to them, "Shall I crucify your King?" The chief priests answered, "We have no king but Caesar." ¹⁶Then he handed him over to them to be crucified.

¹⁷So they took Jesus, and he went out, bearing his own cross, to the place called the place of a skull, which is called in Hebrew Golgotha. ¹⁸There they crucified him, and with him two others, one on either side, and Jesus between them. ¹⁹Pilate also wrote a title and put it on the cross; it read, "Jesus of Nazareth, the King of the Jews." ²⁰Many of the Jews read this title, for the place where Jesus was crucified was near the city; and it was written in Hebrew, in Latin, and in Greek. ²¹The chief priests of the Jews then said to Pilate, "Do not write, 'The King of the Jews,' but, 'This man said, I am King of the Jews.'" ²²Pilate answered, "What I have written I have written."

²³When the soldiers had crucified Jesus they took his garments and made four parts, one for each soldier; also his tunic. But the tunic was without seam, woven from top to bottom; ²⁴so they said to one another, "Let us not tear it, but cast lots for it to see whose it shall be." This was to fulfill the scripture.

"They parted my garments among them,
and for my clothing they cast lots."

²⁵So the soldiers did this. But standing by the cross of Jesus were his mother and his mother's sister, Mary the wife of Clopas, and Mary Magdalene. ²⁶When Jesus saw his mother, and the disciple whom he loved standing near, he said to his mother, "Woman, behold, your son!"

²⁷Then he said to the disciple, "Behold, your mother!" And from that hour the disciple took her to his own home.

²⁸After this Jesus, knowing that all was now finished, said (to fulfil the scripture), "I thirst." ²⁹A bowl full of vinegar stood there; so they put a sponge full of the vinegar on hyssop and held it to his mouth. ³⁰When Jesus had received the vinegar, he said, "It is finished"; and he bowed his head and gave up his spirit.

³¹Since it was the day of Preparation, in order to prevent the bodies from remaining on the cross on the sabbath (for that sabbath was a high day), the Jews asked Pilate that their legs might be broken, and that they might be taken away. ³²So the soldiers came and broke the legs of the first, and of the other who had been crucified with him; ³³but when they came to Jesus and saw that he was already dead, they did not break his legs. ³⁴But one of the soldiers pierced his side with a spear, and at once there came out blood and water. ³⁵He who saw it has borne witness—his testimony is true, and he knows that he tells the truth—that you also may believe. ³⁶For these things took place that the scripture might be fulfilled, "Not a bone of him shall be broken." ³⁷And again another scripture says, "They shall look on him whom they have pierced."

³⁸After this Joseph of Arimathea, who was a disciple of Jesus, but secretly, for fear of the Jews, asked Pilate that he might take away the body of Jesus, and Pilate gave him leave. So he came and took away his body. ³⁹Nicodemus also, who had at first come to him by night, came bringing a mixture of myrrh and aloes, about a hundred pounds' weight. ⁴⁰They took the body of Jesus, and bound it in linen cloths with the spices, as is the burial custom of the Jews. ⁴¹Now in the place where he was crucified there was a garden, and in the garden a new tomb where no one had ever been laid. ⁴²So because of the Jewish day of Preparation, as the tomb was close at hand, they laid Jesus there.

The passion follows naturally from that.

*General Intercessions:*
Jesus' death was his supreme expression of his solidarity with all men and women to bring us all that is good, whatever the cost to himself. So a natural sequence to the passion is *to try to see the world as Jesus sees it.*

For Jesus the world is where God's "glory"—his goodness and greatness—becomes manifest, shared, enjoyed, through our being transmuted by his power into our full selves. But we attain this fullness not just as individuals but also through our living in God's family, all mankind. In these prayers we try to recapture the vision of human solidarity that Jesus died for. We may not have to die for it. Will we henceforth at least *live* for it?

Here we ask God to help all of us in this. After hearing, in the Scripture readings, what God has done for us, it is natural for us to turn to him confidently with our needs. These prayers express our deepest need of all: the realization of God's vision for our human family.

*Veneration of the Cross:*
That suffering, on that particular day in Palestine, and on that particular bit of wood, was for me. It was both crudely human and a full expression of God's faithfulness and love. He fills with his saving power our human efforts, however barren they may seem.

The priest holds up the cross triumphantly, as if at a victory parade. "This is the wood of the cross, on which hung the Savior of the world." We acknowledge that this death *did* fill this executed man with a God-like power to save us from our darkness and dividedness. We kneel in grateful adoration: "Come, let us worship."

*Communion:*
We end with an anticipation of Easter. This is the "body given up for you." In the Our Father, Jesus' prayer "Thy will be done" has a special poignancy for us.

## Reflections
### (especially for parishes with catechumens)

Why not drift with the tide? Wouldn't life be much easier if we let our own comfort and success direct our lives?

Yes, it would be much easier. But many people refuse to be drifters because they believe that if they agreed to be one they'd have no self left.

What happened to Jesus on Good Friday shows us what's involved in being true to myself. It means standing by my beliefs right up to the test of death. My certainty of dying tells me that by a certain time I'll have to get my "act" together and become my true self—if I'm ever going to. In my dying I can put my final seal on the whole endeavor of my life by being true to myself even then.

That's what Jesus did on Good Friday. Like us, he faced the supreme challenge of every human being.

He believed that his true self was to be the bringer of God's kingdom. His death would look like ignominious failure. But he trusted his Father. The night before he died he told his friends: "I will never again drink this wine until the day I drink the new wine in the kingdom of God" (Mark 14:25). Against all the apparent odds, the kingdom *would* come, and he would share in the joy of it.

Tomorrow night the priest will tell the elect how the Holy Spirit will make them more like Christ. The Spirit "will strengthen you to be active members of the Church and to build up the body of Christ in faith and love."

This is the self that the elect and all of us are trying to form in ourselves through responding to God's presence in us. This is what we want to be by the time of our death, so that like Christ and with him we can put our final seal to our true selves then.

"Whoever remains in me, and I in him, will bear much fruit" (John 15:5).

**49**

# EASTER

What happened to Jesus after his death? The only reason Jesus' memory had been preserved at all is the conviction that he "rose from the dead." Christianity has always maintained that if that conviction is false, then "we have nothing to preach and you have nothing to believe." If Jesus' resurrection didn't happen, then "your faith is a delusion" (1 Corinthians 15:14, 17).

Many people miss a lot at Easter by understanding this as mere survival. They imagine Jesus simply coming out of his tomb and living, for a few weeks at least, roughly the kind of ordinary human life he had lived before, with the addition of some special powers of movement.

For an individual to survive death is, of course, wonderful, and, if promised also to us or our friends, great news. But what kind of survival? Is the New Testament simply telling us that we shall resume after our death our present kind of human life, with some special physical powers? What quality will that life have?

How long will it last? How do we obtain it? And can we help others to obtain it?

We shall see that the New Testament tells us two main things about this.

## 1. That credible people claimed that Jesus had risen from the dead and had appeared to them. They were glad to back this claim by making fundamental changes in their whole lives.

About twenty-four years after Jesus' death, St. Paul was writing to the Christian community he had founded at Corinth:

> I passed on to you what I received, that Christ died for our sins, that he was raised to life, that he appeared to Peter and then to all twelve apostles. Then he appeared to more than five hundred of his followers at once, most of whom are alive, although some have died. Then he appeared to James, and afterward to all the apostles. Last of all he appeared to me.

Here Paul is clearly presenting to his friends two kinds of evidence. First, he is telling them what he "received" *from the Christian leaders* between two and six years after Jesus' death (see Galatians 1:18). They had told him then that Jesus' resurrection was the heart of their message, that the whole of their teaching stood or fell by it, and that they were glad to sacrifice everything, including life if need be, to proclaim this message. What we know of them shows that they were level-headed people.

Paul's other kind of evidence is *his own experience:* "Last of all he appeared to me." Like the other Christians he was convinced that the fact that "Jesus is risen" is the heart of the Christian message. Until then he had hated the Christians and vigorously persecuted them. Now "all I want is to know Christ and to experience the power of his resurrection" (Philippians 3:10). Like the others he was ready to sacrifice everything, including his beloved Jewish religion and his life, for that conviction.

The word Paul uses to describe Jesus' appearance makes it plain that the initiative came from Jesus. Jesus showed himself to Paul; it didn't arise from an expectation or wish of Paul's.

To understand what this experience meant for Paul we have to remember what God had promised his chosen people. For more than a thousand years they had experienced him as the God who controls our destiny and wants to bring us all that is good. Again and again, the evil they had done had delayed the coming of his kingship, when he would fully do that. But God had stood by his promise. In spite of so much evil, the kingship would come. The human life we know and treasure would achieve its fullest possibilities. Suddenly, at that climax of human history, an immeasurably fuller, a "resurrected," life would be given.

Then, in the towns and villages of Palestine, a man from Nazareth had announced that that time was virtually here. "Now that I have come, God's kingship is breaking in on you. Look at my healings. Look at my bringing to 'life' the despised, the rejected, the human failures. Above all look at me, and see what you think of the life of someone who is so close to God: the love, the compassion, the freedom, that is the result of that closeness."

Jesus' execution had seemed to be the abject refutation of that claim. God supporting a man so ignominiously executed? Not likely!

*When Jesus showed himself alive to Paul, Paul knew him as having that immeasurably fuller "resurrected" life.* What Jesus had said and done in his lifetime was true. The time when all God's friends would have that promised life was beginning. "Christ has been raised, as the first installment that guarantees that those who sleep in death will also be raised" (1 Corinthians 15:20).

Jesus' resurrection, therefore, wasn't a new life just for him. *It changed the possibilities of life for everyone.* This was the good news that must be told to the whole world! What, more specifically, this resurrection life consists of, we shall examine in the next section.

Paul is the only person whose writings we have who claims himself to have seen the risen Jesus. But the Gospels show that the reason why people believed in Jesus was that others as well had claimed to be first-hand witnesses and that their claims had been convincing enough radically to change people's lives.

We need to be clear how strong must have been the conviction both of the witnesses themselves and of those who believed them in order to get conventional Jews to believe that. To accept that Jesus had risen from the dead as the beginning of the resurrected life for all meant adopting a belief about God's promise of resurrection that was very different from the one they had so far held. The Jews were expecting it to come suddenly, for all, and as the conclusive climax of human history. They were now being asked to believe that in fact it had so far happened *only for one man*, and that the climax for the rest of us was yet to come.

Before long they saw that it also meant their abandoning the religion that meant everything to them, and the loyalties they had so deeply valued.

What experience had led to this? The Gospels make plain that it was that of seeing Jesus risen from the dead and feeling an inner compulsion to proclaim this good news.

Certainly the descriptions of Jesus' appearance in the Gospels vary. Some show Jesus moving among his friends, eating, and asking them to touch him, while at the end of Matthew's Gospel he is more like someone from another world. There is no attempt

to give a consistent or precise picture. How *could* you give a precise picture of experiencing the full power of *God* in a human person?

The atmosphere of hesitancy and fear that comes out in what may be the oldest accounts show that they felt themselves confronted with the God-like. He was still the Jesus they had known so well; yet his life now, though so close and intimate to them, went beyond all their categories of understanding. All you could do was to stammer out what it meant to you. In choosing from so much significance, your own expectations of the resurrection world would no doubt unconsciously guide you. In your telling of it to others, you would be guided by what aspect of your experience you wanted them to understand.

The focus was on the fact that the Jesus they had known is risen. The promised kind of world they had already glimpsed before Jesus' death in his life-style and actions was beginning. This was the good news that *had* to be told. Now we can examine more closely what it seemed to consist of.


## 2. In what they had seen in Jesus, and now in their own lives, they had some experience of resurrection.

We have seen that these ordinary Jewish provincials had an experience of Jesus after his death that persuaded them of two things. First, it convinced them that this was the fulfillment of their hope of God fully coming to his people in the new age of resurrection from the dead. The other conviction was that it was different from how they had expected it: not all entering that age together, but first this man they had known, and then the others through him.

To appreciate the importance of this for us and for everyone, we have to be clear what they meant when they called their experience of Jesus "resurrection." For that we have to look back for a moment at what we saw in the last section.

We saw that their hope of resurrection arose from their whole fourteen hundred years of experience of God. The God they had found in that complex and moving history had always been one who controls the world in order to bring people life, justice, and all that is truly good. Increasingly they had become convinced that this central strand in human history was leading to a climax. Then God would use his *full* power for them. His power was always life-bringing. When that climax came he would fill them with a life that transcends death and all that spoils and limits us as human beings.

Obviously that is a profound yearning in anyone who reflects on his or her situation as a human being. But it tends to be vague. We can long for a human life that transcends all that we experience as harmful and evil, without being able to say what that life would be like.

Then, as we saw, a man from Nazareth had said to people who would listen to him: "Here *is* God coming to you in his full power as he promised. You are seeing it in me. This is the beginning of this new world that you have longed for."

What he was talking about wasn't abstract, vague or fantastic; it was what you saw happening in and through this specific man. It was not just his physical actions, like the healings, or even just the acts of practical and courageous kindness. A man or woman is more than what he or she does, however admirable that may be. At the center of every person is his or her stance to life: the values and purposes that makes that person the man or woman he or she is. It is our choice of these—much more than our particular actions—that make us the kind of people we are.

By far the most striking thing about Jesus was how completely he backed the stance to life of love and service to everyone. This was what he wanted to be. Everything he did and everything he said offered the strongest possible declaration that they alone would be valid and endure. That person, whoever he or she may be, who is trying to be loving and unselfish, isn't like a summer's day that eventually fades into darkness. That kind of life is like God's, as a son is like his father. "God is love, and whoever lives in love lives in union with God and God lives in union with him" (1 John 4:16).

Jesus' backing of love as having absolute validity outraged many and brought him to his death. There's a traitor to the country, despised and hated—a tax collector. No self-respecting

Jew would touch him. "Come to supper," Jesus says to him. "Be my friend."

"How can you possibly condone that tax collector's treachery?" they ask him. His answer was: "Look at God! Surely you know how God acts? Don't we keep the very word 'compassion' exclusively for him? Here is a story about a father who shows that 'compassion' to his prodigal son. Does my story help you remember the way that God acts with us? Does it also suggest to you that my offer of friendship to those bad people isn't despicable but a proof that my complete backing of love shows that *God's kind of world* is here?"

He called it God's "kingship" or "kingdom." An odd kind of kingdom! But for Jesus the only real power was to serve. "If any of you wants to be great, he must be the servant of the rest" (Mark 10:43).

It's so easy to say that, but so difficult to live that—joyfully and warmly! High-principled people can be like blocks of ice. "You want to understand me?" Jesus said. "Well try this story about a shepherd sharing his joy at finding his lost sheep. Doesn't that help you understand the joy you see in me? Or think of a great harvest, or a huge catch of fish, or the finding of an unexpected treasure. Don't they help you to see why you should share in this joy?"

Note that Jesus doesn't say "probably" or "I think." He was absolutely certain that God was in all he did and said.

We know all too well, perhaps, the religious leader who "knows all the answers." In addition, like many such, Jesus' commands were extremely rigorous. Yet he combined this with gentleness, forgiveness, and a total lack of discrimination. The heartless elder son in the prodigal son story, who plainly stands for those trying to frustrate all Jesus' work, is not condemned. The door, at the end of the story, is left wistfully open.

That, if you like, was the "Jesus way." The leading Jews had decided that the Jesus way was subversive and evil; Jesus claimed that it brought you God. His appearance to his friends after his death showed where the truth lay. His way had brought God into our living and our dying and our hope for the future.

The overwhelming impression they had of him now was of intimacy and power. Orientals throw their ideas automatically into pictures. In spite of their deep feeling of intimacy with Jesus—especially at their Eucharists—they pictured Jesus as "above" the world. He had been raised, as Paul said, "to the highest place above"—meaning God's "place." It was their way of saying that he now shared God's power, and not just over them as individuals but over the whole of the human story.

They believed this so strongly because they felt this power in their own lives. It was God's power as he had taught them to recognize it. The only power they had ever seen Jesus interested in was supporting, gentle, liberating: saying "O.K." to your story, as with his publican friends and their own feeling of being forgiven. Above all, it was personal: God's personality in action. You knew yourself healed and forgiven, understood, loved. As you tackled life you knew you could always call "Father." And you knew that this power of his—God's Spirit—would help you tackle it the Jesus way, helping you become a Christ-person.

## And Now?

What would happen now?

They knew that the resurrection world, where a person and his or her promise were secure, had started. They had seen that in Jesus. When would they see it fully in themselves?

Already they were beginning to experience it in their own lives. The joy they felt at seeing Jesus was more than just that felt at recovering a lost friend. Just as before, he was sharing with you his life. Already they felt the joy of that kinship with him when they celebrated it together at the meal he had founded.

When would the full implications appear? What was their own role? How should you use this power to heal and help the people around in that drifting, divided world?

It wasn't until they came up to Jerusalem for Pentecost, seven weeks later, that they began to understand much about that. Then they began to see the practical outcome of Easter for themselves and for the world.

The Church keeps that moment of greater understanding for the day when it came. Not that it is another story: Pentecost is simply the consequence of Easter. But as such it is the founding, the prototype, of the Christian life of each of us. It's our annual reminder of how you and I are being asked to live the Jesus way.

## The Easter Vigil

The Vigil is the main way in which the Church celebrates Easter

**Outline** (not necessarily in this order)

*Service of Light*
    Blessing of New Fire
    Blessing and Lighting of Paschal Candle
    Procession
    Easter Proclamation (Exsultet)

*Liturgy of the Word*
    Up to Seven Old Testament Readings
    Gloria
    Prayer
    Epistle
    Gospel

*Baptisms and/or Renewal of Baptismal Promises by All Present*

*The Eucharist*

**In more detail**

"All the people of Israel are to know for sure that this Jesus, whom you crucified, is the one that God has made Lord" (Acts 2:36).

An oriental "Lord" had great power. Jesus was given God's kind of power, the Holy Spirit. And what the Spirit brings is what he had brought through Jesus in his lifetime: "love, joy, peace, patience, kindness, goodness, faithfulness, humility, and self-control" (Galatians 5:22).

If Jesus' close followers hadn't seen that kind of power or "Lordship" in the risen Jesus, belief in the resurrection would never have captured their minds and hearts. But people had to *believe* those witnesses. They were made more credible by the kind of people they were and what they were prepared to sacrifice for their beliefs. But "the proof of the pudding is ultimately in the eating!" What does it do to someone really to follow Jesus?

Perhaps most of us have had first hand experience of people who follow Jesus in a wholehearted and balanced way. It may be someone who is always a support in need: unobtrusive, selfless, gentle. Or the way of following may be more forthright: the person, say, who risks comfort, success, or even life to be true to himself or herself, or for love of people. A child may hear a lot about love at school, but that will mean nothing to the child if his or her parents show that child no love. So a Christian may hear a lot about the power of the Spirit, but that too will mean nothing without *experience of that power*, given and received.

It is that experience we need to bring with us to tonight's celebration of the resurrection. We need to test each part of the ceremony against our own experiences.

## Service of Light:

### The Fire

At first we see mainly the fire in the darkness. Then the ministers close by it. Then the face and shapes of the congregation flickeringly lit by the weak flames.

This week we have thought a lot about our "darkness." We saw highly respected religious people decide that Jesus must die. We ourselves live in a world overshadowed by violence, mistrust and prejudice. And each of us knows something about the darkness in our own hearts.

While trying to face that fully, as Christians we have confidence. That is what we celebrate above all on this night. We believe:

The Word was the source of life,
and this life brought light to mankind.
The light shines in the darkness,
and the darkness has never put it out          (John 1:4-5).

In this confidence, each of us lets the light of this fire play on our feelings and memories. We may remember, too, as the prayer suggests, that fire also brings warmth and can purify.

The rite takes us behind the cushioned, artificial environment of the modern city to basic and elementary things like light and fire. It also takes us behind the tiny space of time each of us is allotted—for a moment we have before us the overarching structure of creation, as well as the elements that help to make it up. And we see it all as Christ's! "All time belongs to him. To him be glory and power." That was what those to whom the risen Jesus appeared saw in him: Jesus is Lord. He gives sense and light and hope to everything, even the ultimate darkness: death.

## The Procession of the Candle

Will Jesus be that for *me*? Each of us has to work this out in our journey through life together. The procession into the Church reminds us of the journey we share and the light we can receive and give on our way. "Christ, our light!" the priest or deacon proclaims at three stages of the procession. Our reply of "Thanks be to God" can express our deepest feelings about that journey.

## The Easter Proclamation

Then we express our joy in the Easter Proclamation. This is more than happiness or even thanks, though it certainly includes these. As in the Eucharistic Prayer in any Mass, there is a sense of wonder. Our whole self is being addressed by the glorious and awesome. We let our sense of God and what he did through Jesus be stimulated by the light from the candles that we hold, by our being there together, and by the words of the Proclamation:

> The risen Savior shines upon you!
> Let this place resound with joy.

This Proclamation is a song. We don't want to stop the singer after each statement until we've taken in what it means. Instead we let each meteor of poetic imagination rise one after another, while each of us responds to them as we find we want to. This is stately ecstasy, a burst of rejoicing, a song of praise, that makes us pray:

> That Christ shed his peaceful light on all mankind.

### *Reflections*

We appreciate all this more if we remember that this had long been promised. God's promises to his "own dear people" are very moving and help us realize that what happened through Jesus was the culmination of a wise and loving plan (cf. Romans 1:1–2,

"Paul, a servant of Jesus Christ, called to be an apostle, set apart for the gospel of God which he promised beforehand through his prophets in the holy scriptures. . .''). Then consider the following especially:

²The people who walked in darkness
     have seen a great light;
those who dwelt in a land of deep
        darkness,
     on them has light shined.
³Thou hast multiplied the nation,
     thou hast increased its joy;
they rejoice before thee
     as with joy at the harvest,
     as men rejoice when they divide
        the spoil.
⁴For the yoke of his burden,
     and the staff for his shoulder,
the rod of his oppressor,
     thou hast broken as on the day
        of Midian.

*(Isaiah 9:2–4)*

⁶I am the LORD, I have called you
        in righteousness,
     I have taken you by the hand and
     kept you;
I have given you as a covenant to
        the people,
     a light to the nations,
⁷to open the eyes that are blind,
to bring out the prisoners from the
        dungeon,
     from the prison those who sit in
     darkness.

*(Isaiah 42:6–7)*

... he says:
It is too light a thing that you
          should be my servant
     to raise up the tribes of Jacob
     and to restore the preserved of
          Israel;
I will give you as a light to the nations,
     that my salvation may reach to
          the end of the earth.
⁹saying to the prisoners, 'Come forth,
     to those who are in darkness,
          'Appear.'
They shall feed along the ways,
     on all bare heights shall be their
          pasture;
¹⁰they shall not hunger or thirst,
     neither scorching wind nor sun
          shall smite them,
for he who has pity on them will
          lead them,
     and by springs of water will guide
          them.
¹¹And I will make all my mountains
          a way,
     and my highways shall be raised
          up.
¹²Lo, these shall come from afar,
     and lo, these from the north and
          from the west,
     and these from the land of
          Syene.'

                              *(Isaiah 49:6, 9–12)*


Arise, shine; for your light has
          come,
     and the glory of the LORD has risen
          upon you.

²For behold, darkness shall cover the
       earth,
   and thick darkness the peoples;
but the LORD will arise upon you,
   and his glory will be seen upon
       you.
³And nations shall come to your light,
   and kings to the brightness of your
       rising.

*(Isaiah 60:1–3)*


... that the Christ must suffer,
and that, by being first to rise from the dead,
he would proclaim light both to the
people and to the Gentiles.

*(Acts 26:23)*


## Liturgy of the Word:

### Up to Seven Old Testament Readings

These are pictures in our family album. They show us what our human family is like: key personalities that helped to form it and what is happening in it now. Tonight we're looking at our family story in the light of what Jesus has done. The paschal candle, burning there as we hear the Readings, reminds us of that. In these notes we consider the first four of these Readings and look briefly at the last.

*First Picture* (Genesis 1:1–31):

In the beginning God created the heavens and the earth. ²The earth was without form and void, and darkness was upon the face of the deep; and the Spirit of God was moving over the face of the waters.

**65**

³And God said, "Let there be light"; and there was light. ⁴And God saw that the light was good; and God separated the light from the darkness. ⁵God called the light Day, and the darkness he called Night. And there was evening and there was morning, one day.

⁶And God said, "Let there be a firmament in the midst of the waters, and let it separate the waters from the waters." ⁷And God made the firmament and separated the waters which were under the firmament from the waters which were above the firmament. And it was so. ⁸And God called the firmament Heaven. And there was evening and there was morning, a second day.

⁹And God said, "Let the waters under the heavens be gathered together into one place, and let the dry land appear." And it was so. ¹⁰God called the dry land Earth, and the waters that were gathered together he called Seas. And God saw that it was good. ¹¹And God said, "Let the earth put forth vegetation, plants yielding seed, and fruit trees bearing fruit in which is their seed, each according to its kind, upon the earth." And it was so. ¹²The earth brought forth vegetation, plants yielding seed according to their own kinds, and trees bearing fruit in which is their seed, each according to its kind. And God saw that it was good. ¹³And there was evening and there was morning, a third day.

¹⁴And God said, "Let there be lights in the firmament of the heavens to separate the day from the night; and let them be for signs and for seasons and for days and years, ¹⁵and let them be lights in the firmament of the heavens to give light upon the earth." And it was so. ¹⁶And God made the two great lights, the greater light to rule the day, and the lesser light to rule the night; he made the stars also. ¹⁷And God set them in the firmament of the heavens to give light upon the earth, ¹⁸to rule over the day and over the night, and to separate the light from the darkness. And God saw that it was good. ¹⁹And there was evening and there was morning, a fourth day.

²⁰And God said, "Let the waters bring forth swarms of living creatures, and let birds fly above the earth across the firmament of the heavens." ²¹So God created the great sea monsters and every living creature that moves, with which the waters swarm, according to their kinds, and every winged bird according to its kind. And God saw that it was good. ²²And God blessed them, saying, "Be fruitful and multiply and fill the waters in the seas, and let birds multiply on the earth." ²³And there was evening and there was morning, a fifth day.

²⁴And God said, "Let the earth bring forth living creatures according to their kinds: cattle and creeping things and beasts of the earth according to their kinds." And it was so. ²⁵And God made the beasts of the earth according to their kinds and the cattle according to their kinds, and everything that creeps upon the ground according to its kind. And God saw that it was good.

²⁶Then God said, "Let us make man in our image, after our likeness; and let them have dominion over the fish of the sea, and over the birds of the air, and over the cattle, and over all the earth, and over every creeping thing that creeps upon the earth." ²⁷So God created man

in his own image, in the image of God he created him; male and female he created them. 28And God blessed them, and God said to them, "Be fruitful and multiply, and fill the earth and subdue it; and have dominion over the fish of the sea and over the birds of the air and over every living thing that moves upon the earth." 29And God said, "Behold, I have given you every plant yielding seed which is upon the face of all the earth, and every tree with seed in its fruit; you shall have them for food. 30And to every beast of the earth, and to every bird of the air, and to everything that creeps on the earth, everything that has the breath of life, I have given every green plant for food." And it was so. 31And God saw everything that he had made, and behold, it was very good. And there was evening and there was morning, a sixth day.

Here we see two things. One is chaotic and dark. It's there to represent the darkness in each of us, in our families, our other relationships, our world. Left to itself, where would it lead us?

Against that is God's creative Spirit. The Reading makes us *feel* the life and goodness that God's Spirit brings. This opening of the human story as the biblical imagination sees it reminds us of our experience of the beauty and vitality of nature and above all of men and women who are "very good."

The Reading is like a dance or a poem, and at the end of each movement it almost suggests that we clap our hands and shout the refrain: "God saw that it was good."

*Second Picture* (Genesis 22:1–18):

After these things God tested Abraham, and said to him, "Abraham!" And he said, "Here am I." 2He said, "Take your son, your only son Isaac, whom you love, and go to the land of Moriah, and offer him there as a burnt offering upon one of the mountains of which I shall tell you." ³So Abraham rose early in the morning, saddled his ass, and took two of his young men with him, and his son Isaac; and he cut the wood for the burnt offering, and arose and went to the place of which God had told him. ⁴On the third day Abraham lifted up his eyes and saw the place afar off. ⁵Then Abraham said to his young men, "Stay here with the ass; I and the lad will go yonder and worship, and come again to you." ⁶And Abraham took the wood of the burnt offering, and laid it on Isaac his son; and he took in his hand the fire and the knife. So they went both of them together. ⁷And Isaac said to his father Abraham, "My father!" And he said, "Here am I, my son." He said, "Behold, the fire and the wood; but where is the lamb for a burnt offering?" ⁸Abraham said, "God will provide himself the lamb for a burnt offering, my son." So they went both of them together.

⁹When they came to the place of which God had told him, Abraham built an altar there, and laid the wood in order, and bound Isaac his son, and laid him on the altar, upon the wood. ¹⁰Then Abraham put forth his hand, and took the knife to slay his son. ¹¹But the angel of the LORD called to him from heaven, and said, "Abraham, Abraham!" And he said, "Here am I." ¹²He said, "Do not lay your hand on the lad or do anything to him; for now I know that you fear God, seeing you have not withheld your son, your only son, from me." ¹³And Abraham lifted up his eyes and looked, and behold, behind him was a ram, caught in a thicket by his horns; and Abraham went and took the ram, and offered it up as a burnt offering instead of his son. ¹⁴So Abraham called the name of that place The LORD will provide; as it is said to this day, "On the mount of the LORD it shall be provided."

¹⁵And the angel of the LORD called to Abraham a second time from heaven, ¹⁶and said, "By myself I have sworn, says the LORD, because you have done this, and have not withheld your son, your only son, ¹⁷I will indeed bless you, and I will multiply your descendants as

the stars of heaven and as the sand which is on the seashore. And your descendants shall possess the gate of their enemies, [18]and by your descendants shall all the nations of the earth bless themselves, because you have obeyed my voice."

This is a picture of a man responding to what the first picture showed. For him the chief reality in the world is a person who overcomes darkness and chaos and makes things very good.

How can good come out of his sacrificing his only son? Later Jesus must have asked himself: How can my death bring good? I ask the same, in the face of suffering, bereavement, and my own death.

The man in this picture must feel the same painful bewilderment. But stronger even than that is his certainty that God has a greater wisdom and always brings good, even when we can recognize no chance of that.

What we're seeing in this picture is a man joining God as a person: joining most deliberately in all God wants to do for the world.

The result is great fruitfulness.


*Third Picture* (Exodus 14:15–15:1):

[15]The LORD said to Moses, "Why do you cry to me? Tell the people of Israel to go forward. [16]Lift up your rod, and stretch out your hand over the sea and divide it, that the people of Israel may go on dry ground through the sea. [17]And I will harden the hearts of the Egyptians so that they shall go in after them, and I will get glory over Pharaoh and all his host, his chariots, and his horsemen. [18]And the Egyptians shall know that I am the LORD, when I have gotten glory over Pharaoh, his chariots, and his horsemen."

[19]Then the angel of God who went before the host of Israel moved and went behind them; and the pillar of

cloud moved from before them and stood behind them, [20]coming between the host of Egypt and the host of Israel. And there was the cloud and the darkness; and the night passed without one coming near the other all night.

[21]Then Moses stretched out his hand over the sea; and the LORD drove the sea back by a strong east wind all night, and made the sea dry land, and the waters were divided. [22]And the people of Israel went into the midst of the sea on dry ground, the waters being a wall to them on their right hand and on their left. [23]The Egyptians pursued, and went in after them into the midst of the sea, all Pharaoh's horses, his chariots, and his horsemen. [24]And in the morning watch the LORD in the pillar of fire and of cloud looked down upon the host of the Egyptians, and discomfited the host of the Egyptians, [25]clogging their chariot wheels so that they drove heavily; and the Egyptians said, "Let us flee from before Israel; for the LORD fights for them against the Egyptians."

[26]Then the LORD said to Moses, "Stretch out your hand over the sea, that the water may come back upon

the Egyptians, upon their chariots, and upon their horse-men." ²⁷So Moses stretched forth his hand over the sea, and the sea returned to its wonted flow when the morning appeared; and the Egyptians fled into it, and the LORD routed the Egyptians in the midst of the sea. ²⁸The waters returned and covered the chariots and the horsemen and all the host of Pharaoh that had followed them into the sea; not so much as one of them remained. ²⁹But the people of Israel walked on dry ground through the sea, the waters being a wall to them on their right hand and on their left.

³⁰Thus the LORD saved Israel that day from the hand of the Egyptians; and Israel saw the Egyptians dead upon the seashore. ³¹And Israel saw the great work which the LORD did against the Egyptians, and the people feared the LORD; and they believed in the LORD and in his servant Moses.

> Then Moses and the people of Israel sang this song
> to the LORD, saying,
> I will sing to the LORD, for he has
> triumphed gloriously;
> the horse and his rider he has
> thrown into the sea.

Still the same story. God is overcoming the world's darkness, making the world "very good," making the splendor of this known.

Here he begins to do it through a people. The "pillar of cloud" stands for the Jews' experience of his presence with them: splendid, close, supporting. He brings them freedom, a land of their own.

This people's experience of a God whose "glory" consists in giving people freedom and dignity makes them join God, too, in the work we see unfolding. They "put their faith" in God, as Abraham had, or as a husband and wife have in each other, or anyone who joins another deeply in a common aim.

*Fourth Picture* (Isaiah 54:5–14):

5"For your Maker is your husband,
    the LORD of hosts is his name;
and the Holy One of Israel is your
        Redeemer,
    the God of the whole earth he is
        called.
6For the LORD has called you
    like a wife forsaken and grieved in
        spirit,
like a wife of youth when she is cast
        off,
    says your God.
7For a brief moment I forsook you,
    but with great compassion I will
        gather you.
8In overflowing wrath for a moment
    I hid my face from you,
but with everlasting love I will have
        compassion on you,
    says the LORD, your Redeemer.
9For this is like the days of Noah
        to me:
    as I swore that the waters of
        Noah
    should no more go over the earth,
so I have sworn that I will not be
        angry with you
    and will not rebuke you.
10For the mountains may depart
    and the hills be removed,
but my steadfast love shall not depart
        from you,
    and my covenant of peace shall
        not be removed,
    says the LORD, who has compassion
        on you.

**73**

<sup>11</sup>"O afflicted one, storm-tossed, and
    not comforted,
    behold, I will set your stones in
        antimony,
    and lay your foundations with
        sapphires.
<sup>12</sup>I will make your pinnacles of agate,
    your gates of carbuncles,
    and all your wall of precious stones.
<sup>13</sup>All your sons shall be taught by the
    LORD,
    and great shall be the prosperity
        of your sons.
<sup>14</sup>In righteousness you shall be estab-
    lished;
    you shall be far from oppression,
        for you shall not fear;
    and from terror, for it shall not
        come near you."

A husband has angrily parted from his wife. "In excess of anger, for a moment, I hid my face from you. But with everlasting love I have taken pity on you."

We notice the tenderness of this picture. To the husband, she is an "unhappy creature, storm-tossed, disconsolate." So, "with great love I will take you back."

It isn't just his love and compassion, but also his faithfulness:

The mountains and hills may crumble,
but my love for you will never end;
I will keep for ever my promise of peace.

A grudging offer of reconciliation? No, he wants to give her everything.

What kind of story are these pictures showing us? *This* is "the God of the whole earth!"

What is all this leading to? The seventh Reading suggests the answer:

I shall give you a new heart.
I shall put my spirit in you.
You shall be my people
and I will be your God.

## The Epistle (Romans 6:3—11)

This reading takes the story into our own lives. Am I, in my life now, dying to the darkness, chaos, sin in me, so that I live now the new life, the resurrection life, that Jesus has begun? That has been for me the point of the whole story. I could test this by the Readings we've heard tonight:

When I look at the world around me, does it speak to me of God's magnificence, wisdom and love? (1st Reading, about creation)

When I look at myself and God, do I want to share in his great purpose for the world? Do I try to commit myself to him for that with complete trust? (2nd Reading, about Abraham and Isaac)

Do I do this in the way he wants: as a responsible member of his people, chosen to scatter the seed of resurrection justice, freedom, love and joy in the world around us? (3rd Reading, about rescue from Egyptian slavery)

Am I trying to be more aware that this is simply a love story? (4th Reading, about the husband and wife)

To that extent, we are free from the slavery to darkness that threatens us, and "alive for God in Christ Jesus." But Jesus' life shows us that there are no short-cuts or easy answers. If Easter is

**75**

really going to mean anything in my life, don't I need to spend time regularly thinking, praying and perhaps discussing such questions?

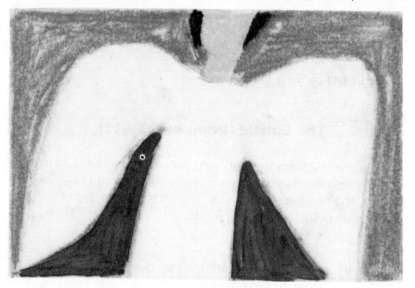

## The Gospel

This changes on a three year cycle as follows:

Cycle A–Matthew 28:1–10:

> Now after the sabbath, toward the dawn of the first day of the week, Mary Magdalene and the other Mary went to see the sepulchre. ²And behold, there was a great earthquake; for an angel of the Lord descended from heaven and came and rolled back the stone, and sat upon it. ³His appearance was like lightning, and his raiment white as snow. ⁴And for fear of him the guards trembled and became like dead men. ⁵But the angel said to the women, "Do not be afraid; for I know that you seek Jesus who was crucified. ⁶He is not here; for he has risen, as he said. Come, see the place where he lay. ⁷Then go quickly and tell his disciples that he has risen from the dead, and behold, he is going before you to

Galilee; there you will see him. Lo, I have told you." ⁸So they departed quickly from the tomb with fear and great joy, and ran to tell his disciples. ⁹And behold, Jesus met them and said, "Hail!" And they came up and took hold of his feet and worshiped him. ¹⁰Then Jesus said to them, "Do not be afraid; go and tell my brethren to go to Galilee, and there they will see me."

Cycle B–Mark 16:1–8:

And when the sabbath was past, Mary Magdalene, and Mary the mother of James, and Salome, bought spices, so that they might go and anoint him. ²And very early on the first day of the week they went to the tomb when the sun had risen. ³And they were saying to one another, "Who will roll away the stone for us from the door of the tomb?" ⁴And looking up, they saw that the stone was rolled back; for it was very large. ⁵And entering the tomb, they saw a young man sitting on the right side, dressed in a white robe; and they were amazed. ⁶And he said to them, "Do not be amazed; you seek Jesus of Nazareth, who was crucified. He has risen, he is not here; see the place where they laid him. ⁷But go, tell his disciples and Peter that he is going before you to Galilee; there you will see him, as he told you." ⁸And they went out and fled from the tomb; for trembling and astonishment had come upon them; and they said nothing to any one, for they were afraid.

Cycle C–Luke 24:1–12:

But on the first day of the week, at early dawn, they went to the tomb, taking the spices which they had prepared. ²And they found the stone rolled away from the tomb, ³but when they went in they did not find the body. ⁴While they were perplexed about this, behold, two men stood by them in dazzling apparel; ⁵and as they were frightened and bowed their faces to the ground, the men said to them, "Why do you seek the living among the dead? He is not here, but has risen. 6Remember how he told you, while he was still in Galilee, 7that the Son of man must be delivered into the hands of sinful men, and be crucified, and on the third day rise." 8And they remembered his words, 9and returning from the tomb they told all this to the eleven and to all the rest. 10Now it was Mary Magdalene and Joanna and Mary the mother of James and the other women with them who told this to the apostles; 11but these words seemed to them an idle tale, and they did not believe them. 12But Peter rose and ran to the tomb; stooping and looking in, he saw the linen cloths by themselves; and he went home wondering at what had happened.

The Gospel reminds us that at the center of all this is ordinary people's experience of the resurrection.

## Baptism

Baptism can take place now. Any adults baptized tonight may be confirmed immediately afterward. The priest has to balance the obvious appropriateness of this against the danger of making the service too long for us.

*We renew our baptismal promises.* This gives me another opportunity of making my own what I have heard tonight: God wants to live in me in my full and free commitment.

- Will I try to overcome the darkness in my relationships with others: my lack of love and of caring?
- Will I try not to be drugged by the easy options and selfish attitudes of an affluent society (Satan's "empty promises")?
- Will I commit myself
     to God as Father and Creator
     to Jesus who is Lord
     to the Spirit who gives life

**78**

especially in and through the Church,
to bring about, where I live, the resurrected world.

For that, may he keep us faithful. Amen.

## The Eucharist

This is *the* Eucharist of the year, the climax of the whole week. For the first Eucharist, Jesus chose, as we saw, the Jews' Passover meal, where they celebrated God rescuing them from evil and giving them life and freedom. Tonight we celebrate his giving us a greater life and freedom.

Perhaps, as we do so, we'll simply want to look back with wonder and gratitude at what we've seen this week.

Not as a story of the past. This week has been about the question of whether our human life really comes to anything.

Our answer has been to open our minds and hearts together—to the kind of life Jesus led and the decisions he faced in the end, and then to people's experience of the outcome, for some in the appearances of the risen Jesus, and for all Christians in his life now, through the Spirit, in our work and fellowship.

"This is the body, given up for you."

"This is the *new* covenant."

*Reflections*
(especially for parishes with catechumens)

The time we've all been waiting for. We could sum up what it means to the elect and the whole parish in nine words:

**From evil**
      **to Life**
            **with the Church**
                  **for Others**

**From evil:** Each of us knows the darkness in our hearts—my failure to face up to responsibility; my not giving someone the love and sympathy he or she needs; my letting anger, fear, prejudice or just sheer selfishness shape my life and my attitudes.

That spoils me as a person. It also helps to spoil the communities I live in: like my family, my place of work, and the local Christian community. We saw how the Service of Light and the Readings (especially the first and third) remind us of this darkness.

But there is hope. Jesus stood out against evil. He went up to Jerusalem. He put responsibility, love and integrity first—and selfishness nowhere! So he died.

From the merely human point of view, that looked like the end of the story. "Love and integrity sound fine. But they don't get you anywhere—except into trouble."

Jesus' resurrection showed that the outcome was entirely different. The outcome of Jesus being true to himself was that "he was raised from the dead by the Father's glory, so that we too might live a new life."

For that, we have to "join him in death." Like him we have to say "no" to selfishness, whatever that may cost us.

Easter says that evil has been conquered. Our lives can have the wholeness, the meaning and the hope that in our hearts we all long for.

But each of us directs our own life. This isn't the kind of decision we make between Ford and Chevrolet, or between Cheer and Fab. It's a life decision.

The priest will ask me this evening:

"Do you reject sin, so as to live in the freedom of God's children?"

Lord, help me to say with my whole heart: "I do."

**to Life:** That's what today is about for the whole parish.

The Readings show that God's plan, from the very beginning, has been simply to give us life: life that is "very good."

It's been a story of our trying to discover the depth of that. God wants us to find just how good that life can be, so that we may have it!

The Old Testament readings showed us that life in action: the strong, simple trust of Abraham, with the great fruitfulness that came of it; the rescue from slavery to freedom; the love and faithfulness of God that directs every moment of the story.

Then there came that one man in whom all this became so tangible. Can anyone really get inside what Jesus did and said without glimpsing a fullness of human life?

And here we are today celebrating the fact that that fullness has been won for us.

It is not won without a journey. In this parish, the elect and the baptized have been sharing in that journey. We have learned together something of what it costs and something of what it gives.

In our meditating on the Scriptures, our sharing in worship, and our support and friendship for one another—especially in our service of others—we've come to know something of what it is to be with Jesus.

Lord, today we celebrate your triumph over death. You won it for us.

It was the supreme proof of your wanting for us all that is very good.

You called us to be the community in which this triumph of yours is especially present in this area.

Today we welcome new members into your community.

Help all of us to be more alive for you in Christ Jesus, so that one day we shall all imitate him in his resurrection.

**with the Church:** God overcomes evil and offers the world life not through a supernatural telex message but through people. Once it was through a man, Jesus. Now it is through the community that represents and embodies Jesus: the Church. That is mainly, in practice, our local church.

We are rediscovering today this fundamental dimension to any full kind of Christian life. The journey we have made with the newly baptized over the last months has helped us see how good it is to learn from each other, and help and support each other. We've found that that's never a one-way process. Everyone, except the very self-complacent, is both giver *and* taker.

The Church wants us to develop this good thing we've been discovering. Between now and Pentecost it asks the faithful to "help the newly baptized to sense the joy of belonging to the community of the baptized" (41.5).

But it doesn't think of it as going only one way. The contribution of the newly baptized is just as vital: "May they enter into a closer relationship with the faithful and bring them renewed vision and a new impetus" (39).

Might that call into question old and cherished ways of doing things? Obviously the Church couldn't have made that request without realizing that it could.

But we know that the Christian community doesn't exist for its own comfort or convenience, but to let the Spirit of Christ live, speak and act in its members, so as to build up Christ's body.

- *We*, this local Christian community, embody Christ for our neighborhood! If the people living here are ever going to

**82**

meet Christ, it will probably have to be through us. What is my attitude to this responsibility?

- What does this responsibility involve with regard to:
  —our needing to know each other better, so as to share this responsibility with one another?
  —a sense of joy. What have we to be grateful and joyful about? Do we show our joy sufficiently, especially to new members: in our services, on our social occasions, in our lives? Do our Eucharists always look and sound like Eucharists (i.e., prayers of wonder and thanks)? What am *I* doing about these things? What more could I do?

- The Church wants the newly baptized to "enter into a closer relationship with the faithful and bring them renewed vision and a new impetus." Is that likely to be easy for them unless the already baptized encourage them? New life is refreshing, but it's also disturbing (ask any new parents). It's easier to run a graveyard then a schoolyard.

  The newly baptized were confirmed when they were "sealed with the Gift of the Holy Spirit." Before they were confirmed the priest or bishop prayed that:

  the promised strength of the Holy Spirit will make you more like Christ,
  help you to be witnesses to his suffering, death and resurrection,
  (and) strengthen you to be active members of the Church and to build up the Body of Christ in faith and love.

**for Others:** God loves *all* men and women. Everyone we meet has a unique and inestimable value and lovableness, and the whole purpose of God's creation is that all this should come to fulfillment.

That is what we pray for when we say: "Thy kingdom come. Thy will be done." We want God's power to break down the ignorance, prejudice and lovelessness that prevent people from recognizing and being their true selves.

"The Church is Christ's body, the completion of him who completes all things everywhere" (Ephesians 1:23).

What about our local church? To what extent do we base our policy in this parish on discovering the needs of the neighborhood and on trying to meet those needs, in cooperation with others? Until quite recently we largely lost sight of this responsibility. The bishops of the world (in the Second Vatican Council) called the Church "a light to all people." Could anything be more worthwhile than helping our own local church be that, realistically and cheerfully, for the people around us?

## Now that we're on the road

Lent and Holy Week have helped us to see the route better.

The Church provides the first signpost: Pentecost. That feast was the completion of Easter. On that day Jesus' friends were shown what it means to be the Easter people, the power they had to bring hope and joy into people's lives and the experience of working with God, out of love for the people around them.

Between now and Pentecost, we could think about what Paul says about the effect of the Spirit in people's lives. For example:

"God has poured out his love into our hearts by means of the Holy Spirit, who is God's gift to us" (Romans 5:5).

"The Spirit makes you God's children, and by the Spirit's power we cry out to God 'Father! my Father!' " (Romans 8:15).

"There are different abilities to perform service, but the same God gives ability to everyone for the common good. The Spirit's presence is shown in some way in each person for the good of all" (1 Corinthians 12:6–7).